I0796268

Foreword by Karen Kingsbury

I remember looking at Emmanuel's sweet face for the first time. My husband, Donald, and I had three biological children, but we felt there was room in our hearts and home for another child. Soon our prayers led us to Heart of God Ministries, an orphanage in Haiti. I remember seeing Emmanuel's photo for the first time and hearing God whisper in my ears, *This one is yours.*

He looked shy and lost and sad, and of course, he was. His parents had died before his first birthday, and his dear grandmother was the only person—the only family—he ever had. Emmanuel's life as a child was a constant walk of faith. Trusting God and trusting the caring, sweet older woman who raised him in those early years.

But when his grandmother grew too sick to care for Emmanuel, he moved to the orphanage. That's where we found him, and where God connected the pieces—the dreams of Emmanuel's grandmother and the plans God had to make those dreams come true.

Indeed, the Lord worked out the details, and in April 2001, we brought Emmanuel home.

In the years since then, Donald and I have watched him grow from that shy little boy who couldn't speak a word of English to a hardworking student and an accomplished athlete. He graduated from Liberty University with a degree in cinematic arts. After graduation, Emmanuel began sharing with us what he called "shadow memories": happy and challenging images and moments from his time with his grandmother in Haiti.

A few years ago, he decided to write a children's book about those memories.

As a #1 *New York Times* bestselling author, I easily could have done the work for him. Interviewed him and written the story myself. But that's not how this worked. Emmanuel wrote every word in this book. After each draft he would share his heartfelt story with me, and I would ask questions, pushing him to go deeper and to give more detail. Asking him to work harder to bring his shadow memories to vibrant life.

That's just what Emmanuel did.

I have tears in my eyes as I write this. Imagine losing your parents as a baby and being raised by your grandmother, only to wind up in an orphanage at age five. Imagine being adopted by a loving family but a family of another color, another culture, from another country . . . even speaking another language.

Emmanuel has been through a lot. But still he remembers the past with a happy heart. He remembers his grandmother and he remembers what God has done for him. He has embraced his life with a joy that challenges me and makes me smile. He loves us. Oh, how he loves us. He is a devoted son and brother and uncle. A loving grandson to my mom and to Donald's father.

I am honored to be Emmanuel's mom.

Emmanuel's story celebrates family and faith and adoption—his and ours. The adoption into the family of God given to us by Jesus' death and resurrection. Share this with your kids and grandkids so they can believe God has a plan for them, too. Share it with your schools and libraries. And remember that Jesus calls us to be like little children. To see our lives with the sort of kindness that Emmanuel sees his.

Way to go, Emmanuel! I love you forever!

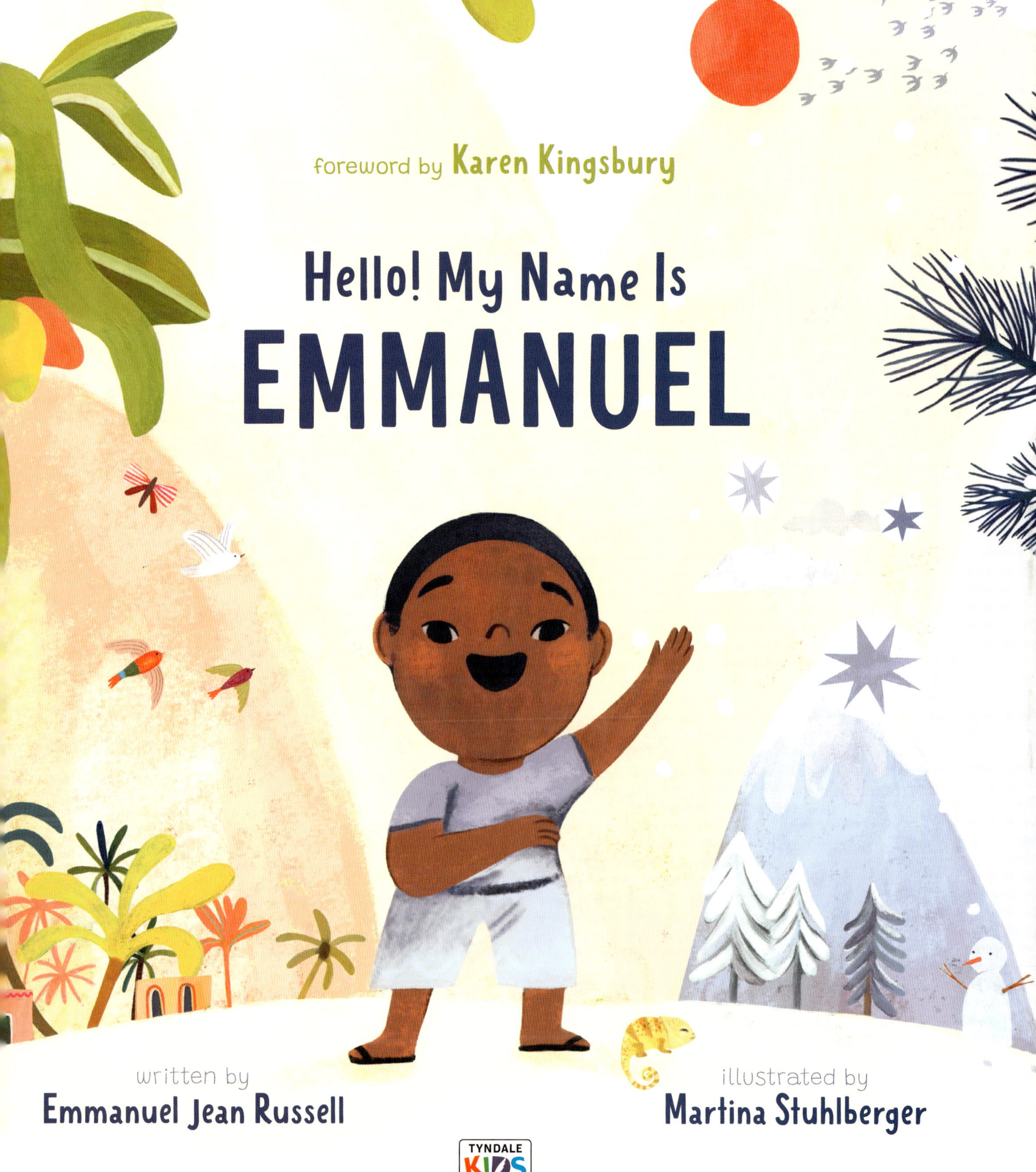

foreword by Karen Kingsbury

Hello! My Name Is EMMANUEL

written by
Emmanuel Jean Russell

illustrated by
Martina Stuhlberger

TYNDALE KIDS

Tyndale House Publishers | Carol Stream, Illinois

I dedicate this book to my grandma in Haiti,
who helped me survive the first three to four years of my life,
and to the family she believed I would find,
who welcomed me with open arms.
But most of all I dedicate this book to the Most High,
Jesus, for His unconditional love!

Visit Tyndale's website for kids at tyndale.com/kids.

Hello! My Name Is Emmanuel

Designed by Jacqueline L. Nuñez

For manufacturing information regarding this product, please call 1-855-277-9400.

For information about special discounts for bulk purchases, please contact Tyndale House Publishers at csresponse@tyndale.com, or call 1-855-277-9400.

Library of Congress Cataloging-in-Publication Data

A catalog record for this book is available from the Library of Congress.

ISBN 978-1-4964-8844-2

Printed in China

31 30 29 28 27 26 25

7 6 5 4 3 2 1

Hello! My name is Emmanuel.

Beautiful: Bèl

I'm six years old, and I live in Washington State. It's beautiful here, especially during the winter. We have snow-covered pine trees and mountains that sky-rocket above the clouds. But I didn't always live in Washington. My story began in a country called Haiti.

When I was younger, I lived in Haiti with my grandma. Grandma told me Emmanuel means "God is with us." I wasn't sure what that meant, but I had a feeling I would understand when I got older.

Grandma took good care of me. She fed me when my tummy grumbled and sheltered me when storms came. She was the best.

My favorite part of the day was when we went to the beach. Almost every day, Grandma and I would walk there before the sun went to sleep. At times it felt like the orange sun was waiting for Grandma and me to sit in our favorite spot.

As I held my grandma's hand, the sun seemed to say goodbye to the island for the day. Grandma would lean over to kiss my forehead and whisper, "Emmanuel, God is with us."

Raindrop: Gout lapli

I told you about my favorite part of the day. Now here's the scariest part. It always felt like the storms waited for nighttime to appear.

The thunder boomed, the lightning flashed, the wind howled. Each one was terrifying. I can still remember raindrops hitting my face from the roof as I tried to sleep.

Grandma prayed to Jesus, which helped me feel safe, even in the storm.

Grandma had the most beautiful dreams. Before sunrise one day, she held me tight in her arms. She told me that in her dream she saw a family from America coming to Haiti to adopt me.

"Emmanuel, I am old and sick. I will not be here forever," my grandma told me. "Adoption is when a child like you needs a home and goes to live with another family. And that family will become your forever family." She smiled. "When that happens, you, Emmanuel, will become their son."

Dream: Rèv

I didn't know exactly what she meant at the time,
but her hug felt like the warm ocean around me.

Each morning, my grandma made sure I started my day right.

She washed my face, my arms, and my feet. It always tickled when she washed my toes.

Mud cake: Galette

For breakfast, we ate mud cakes, which everyone called galettes.

The cool morning breeze from the ocean brushed against our faces. Life in those moments with my grandma felt like it would last forever.

But Grandma had wrinkles on her face, and I could tell time was catching up to her. She acted strong around me, but deep down I knew something was wrong.

One day she looked into my eyes. “Soon, you will go to an orphanage. A place where you will be safe and loved. And after that, God will send you your new family. The one I dreamed about.”

My stomach felt nervous about this. “I don’t want to leave you,” I told her. I felt tears in my eyes.

Again, my grandma smiled. “I will always be with you. And one far-off day we will never have to say goodbye.”

I hugged her waist, and after a minute, the scared feeling drifted away.

One morning, I was drinking fresh coconut milk when I heard my grandma's gentle voice. "Emmanuel," she called out. A jolly man wearing a hat stood there. His smile was brighter than the sun.

Grandma hugged me and whispered, “It is time, Emmanuel. God is with you.” Then she kissed me goodbye. I didn’t know that this was the day I would hug my grandma for the last time. Even now I wish I would’ve held on longer.

The man in the hat helped me into the car, and we drove away. I had never been in a car before. The road was bumpy as we drove over hills and through long stretches of coconut and banana trees.

Finally the man in the hat parked the car.

"This is the orphanage," he said. We stepped out and a pink brick building towered over us. I was so far from my grandma, I was afraid to take even one more step. But the man was kind to me. "It will be okay, Emmanuel," he said. "Follow me."

Before we could go inside, dozens of kids ran up to us. I hid behind the man in the hat. My head felt dizzy, and I wanted to go back home. Then a boy stepped out of the crowd. "Hi! I'm James," he said. He became my friend. But I missed my grandma so much.

A couple hours after I got to the orphanage, James walked with me and the other kids to an outside patio. Some adults were there playing music.

“It is time to worship Jesus,” James told me.

My sadness faded.
This was the same Jesus my grandma always talked about.

Music: Mizik

I looked up, and a million stars seemed to smile at me. God really was with me.

Later that night in my new bed, I felt lonely. But hope bubbled inside my heart. I knew things would get better.

Morning came. "Let's get in line!" James said.

The cafeteria room was packed with kids eager for breakfast. Everywhere I looked, I saw big bowls of food. The smell of rice and beans made my taste buds jump for joy.

Breakfast: Manje Maten

I'd never eaten food like this before.

I smiled at James. "I think I might like it here."

Next, we had school. This made me excited. My grandma used to read to me, but now for the first time, I was going to learn to read and write with other children! I even had my own desk.

The class repeated the Creole alphabet after the teacher: "Ah, An, Be, Se Ach, De."

After school, our class headed to the patio. This area was perfect for hitting mangoes with handmade slingshots. One of the older kids ran up and gave me his.

"Here, Emmanuel. See if you can do it!" He handed me a rock. "Just aim at a mango."

I took the slingshot and rock, and on the third try I actually hit one.

"Good job, Emmanuel," the kids yelled and cheered. "Go get your mango!"

And so I did. It tasted fresh and sweet. This was fun! I still missed my grandma, but I wasn't sad or afraid anymore.

When nighttime spread over the island, we gathered outside again, and everyone started singing to Jesus.

"We do this every night," James told me.

The moonlight was calm on our skin. I smiled at the sky. Somewhere my grandma was looking at the same stars, and that made me happy.

"'Over the mountains and the sea, Your river runs with love for me,'" we all sang.

In that moment, my spirit was full with His love! I knew Jesus really did have a plan for me. No matter where I went, He would go with me, and He would live in my heart forever. Just like my grandma always said.

A few weeks later, the man in the hat pulled me aside after lunch. "Emmanuel, we just got word," he said. "A family from America wants to adopt you." I couldn't believe it!

That night I got my very own soccer ball from my American family. I'd never had anything like this to call my own before.

Many months later, I said goodbye to the orphanage and to my friend James. Soon, a different family would come for him. I held my suitcase tight before getting on the airplane to America. I looked out the window at my colorful, beautiful Haiti. Somehow the island seemed to wave goodbye.

In those last minutes in Haiti, I remembered my grandma's dream. A family from America was really going to adopt me. I was going to have parents and siblings.

Airplane: Avyon

My heart jumped as the plane took off. As I looked out the window, I watched Haiti disappear behind me. I couldn't tell if I was sad or afraid, so I closed my eyes.

I could almost hear my grandma's voice. "God is with you, Emmanuel." I felt myself relax.

Later, sipping on my first soda, I looked out the airplane window and gasped. Something enormous was just ahead of us. I began to yell, “Kisa Sa Ye? Kisa Sa Ye?” (“What is that?”) It was a mountain covered in white. Later, I would learn that the white stuff was snow. I had never seen snow before.

Mountain: Montay

The airplane descended as fast as my beating heart. My stomach dropped, and I grabbed on tight to the man in the hat’s hand.

“That’s normal.” He squeezed my hand. “It’s going to be okay, Emmanuel.”

Finally, we landed in Portland, Oregon. As I got off the plane, I could hear rain falling, and the air stung my face. I'd never felt anything so cold.

My American family stood at the gate with signs. My new mom and dad smiled big. "Hello, Emmanuel!" my dad said. "Welcome home!"

Family: Fanmi

A little boy with blond hair ran up to me. He was about my size. "We have new toys for you."

I didn't understand every word, but I knew this much: my new family loved me.

We drove over the Columbia River to Washington State, my new home. At first, I was shy. But I had a cozy bed with a stuffed black bear. My sister and four brothers quickly became my best friends. I started going to my new school, and over the next few months I learned to speak English.

One night, I looked out at the stars. My heart became warm because I knew this was my grandma's dream. Something told me this new life would be forever.

Eight months have passed since I got adopted, and I've learned something: I love snow! Haiti never gets snow. Not ever. Right now, there's a blizzard coming down. This white fluffy stuff falling from above makes me giggly inside. My siblings and I are going sledding soon!

Sometimes at night I still think about
my grandma, and I thank God for her.
I understand the meaning of my name now.
Emmanuel: "God is with us." God is with me.
He always has been.

Note for Parents

Thanks for reading my story! Adoption is a big part of my family's life, and I love how the Bible reminds us that adoption is important to God too. In Ephesians 1:5 we read, "He predestined us for adoption to sonship through Jesus Christ, in accordance with his pleasure and will." When God adopts us, we become his children!

You might be wondering where you can learn more about adoption, or maybe you feel called to provide support and encouragement to people in need. Here are some resources I recommend:

One Chance Foundation (karenkingsbury.com/onechancefoundation): The One Chance Foundation exists to supply grants to families seeking to adopt. They are passionate about seeing orphans from all over the world brought home to their forever families.

Compassion (compassion.com): Compassion works with thousands of local churches around the world. Each church partner tailors Compassion's holistic child-development model to the contextualized needs of the children in its community, in order to best deliver the whole-life care the children need. If you feel called to sponsor a child, please visit compassion.com.

Skip1 (skip1.org): This organization helps solve world hunger, one skip at a time. They build and renovate kitchens within orphanages and schools in impoverished areas. You can skip something as simple as a five-dollar coffee and donate that money to help feed a child.

He Gets Us (hegetsus.com/en): He Gets Us is a movement to reintroduce people to the Jesus of the Bible and his confounding love and forgiveness. His words, example, and life have relevance in our lives today and offer hope for a better future.

You Were Seen (youwereseen.com): The You Were Seen card—along with a tip where appropriate—lets people know that they matter. They were seen. And the card leads them to the You Were Seen website, where they can access information about the God who sees them every day—the God who is for them and loves them.

Emmanuel Jean Russell is a first-time author who graduated with a film degree from Liberty University in 2019. Emmanuel was born in Haiti and was adopted in 2001. He first lived with his adoptive parents and five siblings in Washington State. In the summer of 2011, Jesus called his family to Nashville. Emmanuel now works for his mother, Karen Kingsbury, running the You Were Seen organization. He loves walking his sweet dog, Molly; playing Spikeball, soccer, and Ping-Pong; and taking in movies with friends. One of Emmanuel's favorite things to do in Tennessee is to sit in a rocking chair on the front porch as a Southern thunderstorm passes overhead. Emmanuel prays that *Hello! My Name Is Emmanuel* will reach orphans, foster kids, and any child who needs to know that God has a purpose and a plan for their lives—and that they have always been a part of his plan, even if they can't see it clearly. To keep up with Emmanuel and see what he's working on next, follow him on Instagram @emmanueljeanrussell19.